Low-maintenance Gardening

Jackie Matthews

HERMES
HOUSE

The edition published by Hermes House

© Anness Publishing Limited 2002 updated 2003..

Hermes House is an imprint of Anness Publishing Limited,
Hermes House, 88–89 Blackfriars Road, London SE1 8HA

All rights reserved. No part of this publication may be reproduced, stored in a
retrieval system, or transmitted in any way or by any means, electronic,
mechanical, photocopying, recording or otherwise,
without the prior written permission of the copyright holder.

Publisher: Joanna Lorenz
Production Controller: Joanna King

Publisher's Note:
The Reader should not regard the recommendations, ideas and techniques
expressed and described in this book as substitutes for the advice of a
qualified medical practitioner or other qualified professional.
Any use to which the recommendations, ideas and techniques
are put is at the reader's sole discretion and risk.

Printed in Hong Kong/China

3 5 7 9 10 8 6 4

CONTENTS

Introduction

CREATING AND MAINTAINING A BEAUTIFUL GARDEN DOESN'T HAVE TO BE TIME-CONSUMING. THERE ARE DOZENS OF WAYS IN WHICH THE VARIOUS COMPONENTS OF THE GARDEN AND THE PLANTING METHODS CAN BE ADAPTED TO MAKE MAINTENANCE EASIER.

Gardens should give pleasure and be places to enjoy. If yours takes up so much of your time in routine maintenance that you have little left in which to really appreciate it, you need to think about how to reduce the labour, without losing out on its beauty.

WHAT IS LOW MAINTENANCE?

Low maintenance does not simply mean cutting down on the number of plants that you grow. The choice of specimens and how you use them is more important – many plants

Above: Ground-cover plants like this prostrate cotoneaster look better than bare soil, and they won't give weeds a chance to grow once they are established.

require hardly any attention from one year to the next. You can also greatly reduce your workload with imaginative design and landscaping.

THE BENEFITS

A modestly sized, low-maintenance garden may require only half an hour a week to keep it looking good. But a truly low-maintenance garden, in which many labour-intensive components such as the lawn or difficult plants have been dispensed with, could require so little work that even if you took several weeks' holiday, it would have little effect on the appearance.

Left: Heathers and dwarf conifers are attractive all year round and need only occasional attention.

Assessing Your Garden

You need to assess which jobs you enjoy and which you dislike, then set about modifying your garden in the order of your priorities and how much time you want to save. If you enjoy propagating but hate weeding, for instance, you need to eliminate the weeds, and if you don't have time to mow the lawn you need to install other surfaces.

Take into account the style of your house and the existing shape and design of the garden itself to make sure that any new feature will fit in and not look out of place.

Check that new plants will grow happily in the soil and position. Some low-maintenance plants such as heathers and conifers have distinct soil preferences for you to consider.

How to Use This Book

Take from this book those ideas that will combine the plants and features you like with the amount of time you want to spend maintaining your garden. In *Easy Garden Maintenance* find out how to make routine jobs less of a chore. *Easy-care Gardens* contains ideas on how different features can be combined to create an attractive garden design needing minimal attention. *Low-maintenance Landscaping* explains how hard and soft features can be used to reduce your workload. *Low-maintenance Plants* provides information on easy-to-grow plants. There is also a section showing how special features, such as a kitchen garden, can be made less time-consuming, as well as a chart to help you select and grow easy-care plants.

Above: *Containers with low-maintenance plants can be used to add interest to areas of paving which also require minimal attention.*

Easy Garden Maintenance

No matter how well designed a garden is, a small amount of routine maintenance will always be necessary, but there are various ways of making many of the regular tasks much less time-consuming and easier to do.

Labour-saving Tools

Using the right tools can save you time and effort, and will make the difference between a job being a pleasure or a chore. Good tools, especially power tools, can be expensive and take up space, so decide which ones will really reduce the time you spend gardening.

Nylon Line Trimmers

These useful tools will cut down long grass around trees, against fences and along edges in no time at all. Many can also produce a trim edge for the lawn much more quickly than traditional shears.

Lawnmowers

If you want to retain a lawn but wish to reduce mowing time, consider buying a mower with a wider cutting width. Rotary mowers are light and easy to use, but unless you are happy to leave the clippings on the lawn, or rake them up, buy one with a clippings collector. The same applies to wheeled rotaries, which many people prefer. For a striped effect a cylinder mower with a rear roller is the best choice, although some other types now have rollers fitted to create a similar effect.

Hedge Trimmers

A powered hedge trimmer will save a lot of time on what is a dusty and unpleasant job if your garden has a lot

of hedge. A mains electric trimmer is the best choice for most small gardens where the hedge is within easy reach of a power supply, but for a large garden a petrol model may be more practical. Battery-powered trimmers are useful for small hedges.

Compression Sprayers

A large-capacity compression sprayer with a long lance is much better for general garden use than a small hand-trigger sprayer if you grow plants that are prone to pests, such as roses and dahlias. As well as pest and disease control, you can use one to apply foliar feeds, and to spray growth inhibitors to reduce the frequency with which you have to cut your hedge as this can be time-consuming. Keep a separate watering can fitted with a dribble bar and shield for weedkiller.

Basic Groundwork

Time spent preparing soil before planting will always pay dividends in the long term in a low-maintenance garden. Soil that is in good condition provides the best possible start for new plants, which will then grow well and be better equipped to withstand attack from pests and diseases. Healthy plants ultimately require less attention than sickly ones.

The first task is to clear all the weeds. If your soil is relatively light and crumbly, these can be physically removed by hand as you dig over the soil. On heavier soil it may be easier to kill the weeds, which you can do by either covering the ground for several months with an impermeable mulch, such as a thick black polythene sheet, or applying a weedkiller.

Digging over the soil opens it up, making it easier for newly planted roots to establish themselves and take up nutrients. Applications of organic matter such as garden compost or well-rotted farmyard manure will benefit all types of soil, improving drainage in heavy soils and water and nutrient retention in light ones.

For an existing bed, a top-dressing of well-rotted organic matter will gradually break down and be taken into the soil by worms.

Digging a New Bed

1 Starting at one end of the bed, dig a trench across it to a spade's depth. Transfer the soil in a wheelbarrow to the edge of the other end of the plot.

2 Tip plenty of well-rotted compost or manure into the bottom of the trench and fork it in.

3 Dig out the next trench, turning the soil into the first trench. Fork organic matter in the new trench, then dig the third one as before. Continue digging trenches and incorporating organic matter until the whole surface of the border has been turned. Fill the final trench with the earth taken from the first one.

AUTOMATIC WATERING

A system that automatically delivers water when it is required will save hours of time every year, and it is better for plants, as they are less likely to suffer from water stress. There are many systems available, so you need to look at several to see which one will be best for your situation.

Most automatic watering systems are fitted with a suitable control system to reduce the pressure, and act as a filter.

Some systems are controlled by the moisture level in the soil, but most operate on a continuous drip basis. Drip feed systems are versatile enough to be used for plants in beds, borders or in containers. Use a T-joint to run branches or tubes for individual drip heads. A timing device will turn your watering system on and off automatically, yet can easily be deactivated if the weather is wet.

Above: Leaky pipe and perforated hose systems are suitable for beds and borders where they can be hidden.

Unless your garden is very small, it is best to install a pipeline buried just beneath the ground surface, then you can "plug in" various watering devices as necessary.

Leaky pipe and perforated hose systems are suitable for beds and borders or the kitchen garden. You can bury them beneath the surface or lay them on top of the soil.

Above: A pop-up sprinkler can be set into the lawn. The head is pushed up out of the ground by the water pressure when the tap is turned on.

Above: A drip feed system is ideal for hanging baskets and window boxes. It will eliminate the daily chore of watering by hand.

Above: Apply a slow- or controlled-release fertilizer to established plants in spring or early summer.

LOW-MAINTENANCE FEEDING

This really does pay dividends. If you see a garden with particularly lush and healthy-looking plants, the chances are they have been well fed.

Slow- and Controlled-release Fertilizers

If you use modern slow- or controlled-release fertilizers, you can feed your plants just a couple of times a year. Both allow the nutrients to seep out into the soil over a period of months but controlled-release fertilizers are affected by soil temperature. Nutrients are only released when the soil is warm enough for growth. Use a hose-end dilutor for applying a soluble fertilizer.

Feeding Beds and Borders

Most established plants, but especially demanding ones like roses, benefit from an annual feeding. Apply a slow- or controlled-release fertilizer in spring or early summer, sprinkling it around the bushes. Keep it away from the stem, sprinkling it further out where most of the active root growth occurs. Hoe it into the surface then water it in, unless rain is expected, to make the fertilizer active more quickly.

Feeding the Lawn

The quickest way to feed your lawn is with a wheeled spreader. Individual models vary, but you can usually adjust the delivery rate. Test the rate on a measured area of path first, then sweep up the fertilizer and weigh it to ensure the application rate is correct.

Feeding Container Plants

Plants grown in containers require supplementary nutrients to keep them healthy. You can mix controlled- or slow-release fertilizer granules into the potting soil when you plant, or slip sachets or pellets beneath individual plants as you plant them.

Above: Container plants need additional feeding such as this slow-release pellet.

REDUCE WEEDING

It is entirely possible to have a beautiful garden where weeds are seldom a problem. The trick is to not allow any space where they can gain a major hold. Reducing the amount of bare earth in your garden and introducing more hard landscaping will reduce the area that weeds can grow in.

In beds and borders dense planting and ground cover will blanket the ground so well that weeds are unlikely to gain a foothold. Where young plants have not yet reached their maximum spread, applying a mulch to patches of bare earth will ensure that weeds cannot grow.

Using Weedkillers

Pulling up perennial weeds by hand is time-consuming and often ineffective as they usually grow again unless you remove every piece of root. Digging

Above: A contact weedkiller applied through a dribble bar will be useful for clearing a large area that has been overrun by perennial weeds. You may need to shield adjacent plants from the spray.

Above: Difficult and perennial weeds, like this ground elder, can be killed by painting on a translocated weedkiller.

them up may not be possible in an established bed or border, and you may have to resort to a contact weedkiller. Beware, as most weedkillers will kill or damage whatever they come into contact with.

Deep-rooted perennial weeds, such as bindweed, can be very difficult to eradicate and are best treated by painting on a translocated weedkiller, such as one based on glyphosate. Other contact weedkillers may not kill all the roots, but this chemical moves to all parts of the plant.

> GARDENER'S TIP
>
> Paths can easily be kept weed-free for a season by using products sold for the purpose. A single application will quickly kill existing weeds and prevent the growth of new ones for many months. Use an improvised shield to prevent the weedkiller being blown on to the flowerbeds.

Above: Gravel makes an attractive sur-face, and can be weed-free with very little effort.

MULCHES FOR GROUND COVER

A mulch is a layer of material that will cover the ground completely to sup-press weeds and conserve moisture in the soil by preventing loss of water through evaporation. It can be purely functional or it can be decorative, and it can be organic or not. Always prepare the ground thoroughly before applying a mulch, taking care to elim-inate perennial weeds and work in plenty of organic material such as well rotted manure or garden compost. Make sure the ground is wet before applying a mulch; soak it first if necessary.

Loose Mulches

Most loose mulches, such as chipped bark, cocoa shells, gravel, garden com-post and rotted manure, are more visually appealing than sheets, and the organic ones rot down to improve the soil's structure and fertility. They need to be applied about 5cm (2in) thick.

Sheet Mulches

Woven plastic mulching sheets are effective and economical, but unattractive. However, they can be used in combination with a decorative loose mulch, which can then be applied more thinly than the recom-mended depth. Sheet mulches are use-ful for low-maintenance shrub beds and newly planted trees, both of which can be left undisturbed for sev-eral years, and are best used when the bed or border is to be newly planted.

PLANTING THROUGH SHEET MULCH

1 Make a slit around the edge of the bed with a spade, and push the sheet into this.

2 At each planting position make a cross-shaped slit in the sheet. Fold the flaps open to plant, then fold back in place. Small plants can be planted using a trowel, but for shrubs you will need to use a spade.

Easy-care Gardens

SOME GARDEN STYLES LEND THEMSELVES PARTICULARLY WELL TO LOW-MAINTENANCE GARDENING. THEY OFTEN RELY ON A VISUALLY PLEASING USE OF HARD LANDSCAPING ELEMENTS COMBINED WITH A MINIMUM OF WELL-CHOSEN PLANTING.

A MINIMALIST GARDEN

It is possible to create a striking garden using very little at all. The garden elements can be pared down to the absolute minimum and anything fussy, distracting or unnecessary can be excluded from the scheme.

A garden that relies on minimal planting will be the most labour-saving of all, but you need to choose carefully. The few plants used must work hard to earn their place there.

Using Space

Form and space are what matter in a minimal design. Anyone embarking on such a totally labour-saving design will need an eye for shape and contrast, so that the garden is pleasing to the eye, yet uncluttered.

The design will rely on the clever use of space, defined by a few strategically placed features, such as pots, stones, statues or plants, or a bold architectural feature such as a wall.

Above: The painted wall and gravel act as a foil to the carefully selected foliage plants in this striking area.

Left: Strong architectural features, such as the brick wall, unadorned pergola and symmetrical oblong planter, are typical elements of a modern garden.

Simple dramatic juxtapositions can create sufficient interest. For instance, a paved or gravelled area can become a visually pleasing space with the addition of just a few carefully sited large pots containing some architectural plants, or perhaps a raised bed or pool. Pebbles or boulders can be used to add extra texture, and perhaps some flowering annuals will add a splash of summer colour.

Adding Colour

Colour in the form of painted surfaces can also be used for impact in a minimalist garden, perhaps on a large wall or the edges of a raised bed. It can be used to complement planted gravel or an expanse of paving.

Above: A striking individual plant such as this easy-care bamboo in a pot is complemented by the adjacent pebbles.

Positioning Plants and Pebbles

A few good plants can go a long way if they are carefully positioned to create form in an open space. They need to be dramatic in shape or colour so that they make an impact on the design. Architectural plants such as phormium, yucca, bamboo clumps or even small trees all work well, especially when used in isolation.

Pebbles are also a good way to introduce additional texture. They work particularly well in areas of paving or with potted plants.

Left: Form is paramount in this dramatic garden comprising a series of integrated islands.

GRAVEL AND PAVED GARDENS

Gardens that rely heavily on paving or gravel instead of lawn can be virtually maintenance-free. They need to be well planned, however, to avoid them looking oppressive and harsh. The solution is to include a variety of materials to create contrasting shapes and textures, and to complement this with the planting. Even the simplest of designs can be transformed into a garden full of charm and character.

Designing with Hard Materials

Different materials can be used effectively to divide a large area into smaller sections, creating interest through changes of texture, and even height if you introduce features such as raised beds.

Formal structures usually work best for paving, especially in a space bounded by walls. Bricks can be laid in attractive patterns, adding colour and warmth to a design. The small dimensions of bricks will create satisfying contrasts when juxtaposed with large paving slabs. Granite setts, cobbles and brick or clay pavers can also be laid in interesting patterns.

Gravel, which has a softer texture than hard paving, adds another type of contrast. It works with both formal lines and informal designs as it lends itself to curves. There are lots of different gravels available in many colours and grades. Choose one, or several, that will suit your design.

Above: Gravel is a sensible alternative to grass and will look good when used with the right plants and accessories.

Left: A raised central planting area and water features in this paved garden have been constructed from contrasting materials.

Additional Features

Including other features in paving or gravel gardens adds yet more interest. Ponds or fountains introduce the element of water. Statues, large containers and even benches all make excellent focal points.

Incorporating Plants

Beds and borders can easily be incorporated into gravel and paved gardens. If you do not want to be bothered with maintaining large planting areas, you can create small filled spaces within the gravel or paving.

Beds can be filled with some low-maintenance ground-cover plants, but focal plants may also be desirable to draw the eye, especially during winter. Architectural plants, such as

Above: Even the tiniest area can become a gravel garden.

Cordyline australis (for warmer winters) or *Yucca gloriosa* (for cooler areas), work well as focal plants. Clipped box (*Buxus sempervirens*) is useful for formal designs. Two or three clips during the growing season are sufficient to keep it in shape.

Containers are another option, but they will require daily watering in summer unless you install an automatic watering system.

Above: Paving constructed in an interesting design becomes an extra feature in the garden.

GARDENER'S TIP

The pattern to which bricks and pavers are laid alters the overall impression created when viewed en masse. The stretcher bond is most effective for smaller areas and for paths. Herringbone is suitable for both large and small areas. Basket weave needs a reasonably large expanse for the pattern to be appreciated.

A JAPANESE GARDEN

True Japanese gardens require very little maintenance as the components are mainly easy-care features such as gravel, pebbles, stones, wood, water and occasional, carefully-chosen and well-positioned shrubs or small trees.

Designing the Garden

A sense of tranquillity and areas for contemplation are important elements in a Japanese garden. The design must be kept simple and uncluttered, concentrating on outline, shape and contrasting surface textures, while the use of plants is restrained, resulting in a garden that satisfies the senses but requires mimimum aftercare.

Focal Points

Rocks and stones have a special importance in many Japanese gardens. They can be set in an area covered with fine pebbles, which are an ideal labour-saving ground cover. When wet, they change colour and catch the light.

Choose some special stones of varying size, colour and character, and arrange them asymmetrically in one or two areas in uneven numbers. Traditionally, the pebbles are raked into variations of parallel lines and snaking spirals centralized on the main rock features. Gravel can be substituted for pebbles as a cheaper option.

Above: Strategically placed large stones are an intrinsic and symbolic feature of a traditional Japanese garden. They are said to focus the mind for contemplation.

Left: A classic Japanese-style garden is simple and uncluttered with various harmonious focal points.

PLANTS FOR A JAPANESE
GARDEN
Acer palmatum
Azalea
bonsai trees
camellias
dwarf bamboos
Iris ensata
moss
small pines

You can inset a walkway of large paving slabs or sawn tree-trunk pieces in the gravel.

Minimal Planting

In an authentic Japanese stone garden the only plants might be mounds of green moss providing a softening contrast with the stones and rocks, but other types of Japanese-inspired garden include a few more plants, chosen for their interesting form or grace. These can be planted through the pebbles or in large simple containers.

If mosses, which thrive in moist conditions out of direct sun, cannot be encouraged to grow, try moss-like plants as an alternative, such as *Sagina subulata*, *S. procumbens*, or, in mild areas, the ground-hugging carpeter *Soleirolia soleirii*.

A Water Feature

Water, the essence of life, should always be present. In a real Japanese garden, it would be fresh running water, but for the low-maintenance gardener even a bowl filled with water

is calming in a garden and offers birds the opportunity to drink. A bubble fountain washing over pebbles or a running stream effect would be ideal.

Traditional Ornaments

In eastern philosophy, traditional garden features have their own significance within the strict rules and special meanings of the garden design. Bamboo wind chimes create soothing sounds, while a rounded lantern and a linear bridge are pretty, and useful for introducing contrasting shapes. You could introduce different ornamentation to suit your own preferences, with the purpose of providing contrasting shapes and colours.

Above: Bamboo, smooth pebbles and rounded water features are ornamental and require little attention.

A Hot and Colourful Garden

The kind of garden that is inspired by the Mediterranean countryside is packed with tough, self-sufficient plants that are colourful, attractive to bees and butterflies and wonderfully scented. It may also stock many aromatic edible plants that are useful for the kitchen. You might start off with a small patch or bed, but the benefits of this style of labour-saving garden are such that you may consider converting a larger area.

Mediterranean plants are resilient and drought-resistant. Their constant adaptations for survival in hot, arid areas – aromatic vapour, shimmering foliage, tough or spiny leaves and silvery hairs – also make them unappealing to pests, and their tough constitutions help them to resist disease.

Basic Groundwork

All the above make Mediterranean plants ideal candidates for a low-maintenance garden, as long as the ground is prepared so that they will thrive in temperate climates.

You will need to add plenty of grit or gravel to the soil to give it sharp drainage so that the plants do not have to struggle to survive in wet, compacted

Above: The graceful spring flowers of Tulipa sylvestris *and grape hyacinth grow amongst rosemary and lavender, just as they would in the wild.*

Left: Lavender, Cistus, Euphorbia *and asphodels make their distinctive mark on a gravel bed in summer.*

Left: This herb garden is full of leaf and vibrant colour a mere 15 months after planting.

There is no need to add fertilizer or manure when planting. Most Mediterranean plants are adapted to grow in poor soil, and if it is too rich they will produce weak, sappy growth. In poor soil they will generally grow tougher and flower more freely.

Simply cover the surface of the soil with gravel and water the plants well until they establish themselves. After their first season, you will not need to water them. In severe summer drought, you can revive any stressed plants by dousing them with water; if watering is impractical, cut back the plants severely and they should revive.

ground, where they would inevitably rot as their roots need dry conditions.

A top layer of gravel or stones will work as moisture-retaining mulch that also keeps foliage crowns dry and absorbs heat for the benefit of the plants.

Designing the Garden

This kind of garden requires no planning to ensure the colours and textures complement one another. The plants naturally team well, forming a magical tapestry of wonderful partnerships.

The predominant shrubs and sub-shrubs are evergreen, with grey and silver tones, sustaining the garden through the quieter winter months. In spring, flowering bulbs pop up in bright reds and yellows. Summer explodes with foliage and flower.

Suitable Planting

Select only those types of plant that will survive with minimal attention and enjoy the sharp draining conditions of your garden.

Containers

Following the age-old Mediterranean tradition of growing special plants in pots you can grow a few brightly coloured geraniums against a white-washed wall, or perhaps a fig tree if you have a very sunny, sheltered corner in the garden.

MEDITERRANEAN PLANTS

Artemisia absinthium
Cistus
Cytisus
Eryngium
Euphorbia
Lavandula
Rosemarinus
Salvia officinalis
Thymus

A Wildflower Garden

An established wildflower garden requires much less maintenance than a conventional one. Making one, however, can initially be quite demanding as there is some basic preparation of the soil required and the garden takes time to become established. Creating a large meadow will need much more effort, so it is advisable for the time-pressed gardener to concentrate on a small wildlife swathe.

Planting a Border

The simplest way to grow wildflowers is in an existing border, either on their own or with some other herbaceous plants and shrubs. This can work especially well if you combine wildflowers with the many garden plants that are forms of wild flowers, such as carpeting *Ajuga reptans* and self-seeding poppies and forget-me-nots.

Wildflowers can be sown or planted in the same way as other plants, but they will not thrive in ground that is fertilized.

Above: Once a threatened species, yellow cowslips (Primula veris) *are now quite widely seen in wild areas.*

On cultivated ground the ranker weeds tend to take over and smother the plants you want to encourage, so it is worth clearing the area of weeds first. Then you can sow the wildflower mixture or plant out perennials in the spring.

Colonizing a Lawn

You can scatter the wildflower seed directly over the area, but the competition from the grass will be intense. For better results, sow the seed in trays, prick out and grow the plants in pots first. Plant them out in spring, when the perennials are strong enough to compete with the existing grass.

Once the perennials are established, they will self-sow, which is always more successful than simply scattering seed yourself.

PERENNIALS FOR WILD-
FLOWER PLANTINGS

Achillea millefolium
Ajuga reptans
Campanula rotundifolia
Cardamine pratensis
Centaurea scabiosa
Fritillaria meleagris
Geranium pratense
Monarda fistulosa
Primula veris
Ranunculus acris

Converting a Field

If you are lucky enough to have a field and want to turn it into a wildflower meadow, your task is much harder. Before you can start sowing or planting wildflowers you will need to spend a whole year mowing the grass at regular intervals to keep it short. This will kill off most of the more invasive grasses, and leave only the finer ones. When the grass is under control, you can proceed as for a lawn.

Clearing New Ground

For those with a smaller area to convert, another effective method for establishing a wildflower area is to clear it completely, removing all traces of perennial weeds. Then sow a wildflower and grass seed mixture formulated for your area, as for a border. There are several suppliers for this type of seed.

Above: Cornflowers are a delightful addition to a wildflower garden with their intense lavender colouring.

Maintaining Wildflowers in Grass

Wildflowers growing in grass should be cut once or twice a year. The best time is in summer once the main flush of plants have seeded. Remove the cuttings to prevent feeding the soil.

Above: Create a tranquil summer haven within the informal splendour of a wildflower garden filled with colourful plants.

Low-maintenance Landscaping

YOU CAN ARRANGE YOUR GARDEN AND MODIFY THE WAY YOU PLANT
BEDS AND BORDERS SO THAT VERY LITTLE REGULAR MAINTENANCE
WILL BE REQUIRED. YOU CAN ALSO MAKE YOUR GARDEN MUCH MORE
INTERESTING IN THE PROCESS.

*Above: Mixing hard landscaping materials
and plants breaks up a large area of lawn
and prevents it looking dull.*

THE GARDEN FLOOR

The greater part of most traditional
gardens is given over to a large
expanse of lawn, which is often edged
by a path or a small area of paving.
Lawns are time-consuming and expensive to maintain in good condition,
and they can be boring. There are
ways of keeping mowing to a minimum, but anyone wishing to cut down
drastically on the labour involved
should consider alternative surfaces

such as gravel or paving for at least
part of the area normally covered by
the lawn.

SIMPLER LAWN MAINTENANCE

If you want to keep a lawn there is a
lot you can do to reduce mowing time
to a minimum. Upgrading your lawnmower to a more powerful or wider
cutting one is the most obvious, but

*Above: This garden has been mainly
planted with large shrubs that require
miminal attention, leaving only a small
central area of lawn that will not take
long to mow.*

GARDENER'S TIP

Wider mowers cost more but will save mowing time for a larger lawn. For a tiny lawn, however, the extra manoeuvrability of a smaller mower can be important if there are few long straight runs.

eliminating fussy beds and curved edges to borders might speed things up by allowing you to mow in straight lines. There are also other approaches to try. Alternatively, keep just a small area of lawn, and plant ornamental grasses, ground-cover plants or shrubs over the remaining area.

Trimming Edges

Unsightly untrimmed edges can make a garden look untidy, but trimming with shears, long-handled or ordinary, is tedious and time-consuming. If you have a lot of these to trim, invest in a powered lawn edge or nylon line trimmer with a swivel head, which can be

Above: Replacing lawn with low-maintenance plants will reduce mowing time.

used for this job as well as scything down persistent weeds. It is best to buy the sturdiest you can afford as the lighter versions can prove less economical in the long term.

Multi-level Mowing

Another way to reduce the amount of time spent mowing is to cut different parts of the lawn at different intervals, leaving some areas to grow longer. This involves cutting broad "pathways" regularly, and mowing other areas every second or third time with the mower blade set higher giving a more natural appearance. You can leave some grass uncut except for a couple of cuts a season, but it will probably need to be cut with a nylon line trimmer instead of a lawnmower.

Above: A nylon line trimmer will enable you to trim lawn edges with considerable speed.

MAKING A MOWING EDGE

Edging the lawn with brick or paving, so that the mower can run over it saving time and evergy, means that the only trimming you will need to do will be occasionally cutting back any long stems of grass that grow over the paving.

1 Lay paving slabs or bricks on the grass for positioning, and use a half-moon edger (edging iron) to cut an edge.

2 Slice off the grass with a spade and remove soil to the depth of the pavers, plus several centimetres (a couple of inches). Lay a sub-base of sand and gravel mix, and consolidate it using a piece of wood and a mallet.

3 For paving slabs, use five blobs of mortar for each slab, and lay them on top, then tap them hard, using a mallet. Bricks will just need a small blob of mortar under each.

4 Make sure the slabs are flush with the lawn, and use a spirit level to check that the slabs are laid evenly. Mortar the joints for a neat finish, otherwise unsightly weeds will grow in them.

GARDENER'S TIP

Choose a paving or brick colour that will blend well with the adjacent border. Creeping plants will soon extend over the surface to soften the effect.

ALTERNATIVES TO GRASS

If you like a green lawn, but don't enjoy or have time for regular mowing, you could consider a grass substitute. Those mentioned here are fine for occasional foot traffic and as a visual focal point, but they won't stand up to the hard wear of a children's play area like grass will.

There are other drawbacks to using grass substitutes for lawns. You won't be able to use selective lawn weed-killers on them, so you will have to hand weed as necessary for a season or two, until the plants have knitted together. Beware of common stone-crop (*Sedum acre*), an attractive yellow-flowered carpeter sometimes sold as a grass-substitute. It may become a serious weed in your garden.

Thyme

A quick spreader with attractive foliage and flowers, thyme makes a good grass substitute and is aromatic

Above: Romantic and unusual, chamomile is quite hardy and will last for many years.

when crushed. Culinary thyme (*Thymus vulgaris*) is too tall, so use a carpeter like *T. pseudolanuginosus* or *T. serpyllum*.

Chamomile

Another aromatic plant for lawns is chamomile (*Chamaemelum nobile*, syn. *Anthemis nobilis*). Look for the variety 'Treneague', which is compact and does not normally flower.

Clover

If clover is a problem in your lawn, it may make a good grass substitute. Once established it will keep green for most of the year and will tolerate dry soils. You'll only have to mow a couple of times a year, after the flowers appear, to keep it looking smart.

Above: Swathes of thyme make an eyecatching and fragrant alternative to a lawn.

GRAVEL

Decorative gravel is an excellent, inexpensive but practical garden surface. It is attractive, trouble-free, easy to lay and harmonizes well with plants. It will conform to irregular outlines, and it can be effective in a large or small area. Whole gardens can be turned over to gravel with some judicious use of complementary paving and attractive planting. An edging is a good idea, otherwise the gravel will become scattered into surrounding areas.

Many garden centres and stone or builders' merchants sell a wide range of gravels in different sizes and colours. You will find the appearance changes according to the light and whether the stones are wet or dry.

Above: Curves present no problems for gravel. Using edging will keep the gravel in the right place.

Above: Gravel makes an attractive background for plants and needs minimal maintenance.

Making a Gravel Bed

You can set a gravel bed in a lawn or within an area of paving. In a large lawn a winding ribbon of gravel, designed to imitate a dry river-bed, can look very effective. If the garden is smaller, a more compact shape, perhaps oval or kidney-shaped, may be more appropriate.

Cut out a shape using a half-moon edger (edging iron) and remove the turf about 10cm (4in) deep with a spade. If you want to grow drought-loving plants, dig in plenty of coarse grit. For growing more hungry plants, add well-rotted manure or compost. The gravel needs to be about 5cm (2in) deep. Keep the gravel well below the surface of the lawn, otherwise it will spill on to the surface of the lawn and damage the mower. Choose a size that will be noticeable if it does stray.

Large Gravel Areas

For anything larger than a small island bed, consider laying a plastic sheet over the area to suppress weed growth. If the gravel garden is low-lying or in a hollow, provide a sump for excess water to drain into. Ensure that the surface is quite smooth before laying the sheet, and overlap the joints. Tip the gravel over the plastic sheet and rake it level to make a 5cm (2in) layer.

Planting in Gravel

Many plants will grow well in a gravel bed, but for a low-maintenance garden choose drought-resistant plants that won't need watering, even in dry spells. Scoop back the gravel and plant normally, but avoid planting too

deeply and keep the gravel away from the immediate area around the stem.

If planting through a plastic sheet, scoop back the gravel then make cross-slits through the plastic. Enrich the soil with garden compost or fertilizer and plant normally. Fold back the sheet and replace the gravel, taking care not to cover the crown of the plant.

Above: A recently planted gravel bed within a lawn is already showing plenty of colour. The plants will soon spread to cover much of the gravel.

Right: Soft mounds of thyme planted in a gravel area soften the effect, adding colour and contrasting textures.

Paving

A paved area needs practically no maintenance, just an occasional brush and every few years a blast with a high-pressure water jet. As well as being labour-saving it should contribute positively to your garden design, linking and complementing other elements of the garden.

Creating Effects

Builders' merchants and many garden centres stock a variety of attractive paving materials to suit most tastes and styles, and these can be laid to create all sorts of patterns, formal or informal. As well as different materials, surfaces can vary in texture. Big slabs are suitable for large areas, while bricks and pavers are better for small areas. A mixture of different paving materials will introduce variety and interest to a scheme.

Above: Builders' merchants stock a variety of paving materials. Choose those that will complement other elements in the garden.

Concrete Paving Slabs

Large slabs made from concrete are a popular choice for patios, paths and drives. They come in a range of sizes, textures and colours, and are easy to lay once a solid foundation has been prepared. Slabs, especially circular ones, are suitable for use as stepping stones set in a lawn or in gravel.

Natural Stone

Although this looks splendid, it is very expensive and difficult to lay. It can be dressed, that is cut into regular shapes with smooth edges, or random, with irregular outline and thickness. The latter is suitable for crazy paving and looks much better than broken concrete fragments.

Bricks and Pavers

Concrete or clay pavers and bricks are very striking when they are laid in small areas. They are especially suitable for visually linking the garden to a brick house. They can be laid in

Above: This crazy-paved area is softened by the addition of container-grown plants.

to be only 5–10cm (2–4in) thick for foot traffic but about 15cm (6in) if vehicles are to be driven over it. Concrete and brick paving slabs can be bedded on mortar, but clay pavers must be bedded on sharp sand using a plate compactor.

Plants and Paving

A few strategically placed plants will greatly improve the appearance of the paved garden without requiring too much extra work.

Plants in beds alongside the paving can be encouraged to fall on to the paving to soften the hard edges. Containers are useful, too, to break up a large expanse, or to introduce colour where there is no bed for planting in. But if you design the paving with integral planting areas or raised beds, the plants will need less watering than they would in containers.

intricate designs. Pavers come in a wide range of sizes, colours and thicknesses and have different finishes.

Laying Paving

Paving needs to be laid on to a firm base. The area will have to be excavated to a depth that allows for hardcore, mortar and paving. Hardcore needs

Above: You can create planting spaces in paving by removing slabs to expose the soil below. A stone mulch disguises the soil and prevents it splashing on to the paving.

Left: Combining different types of paving will add considerably to the visual impact and interest.

29

BEDS AND BORDERS

Attractive, well-filled beds and borders bring a garden to life, but they are potentially time-consuming. You can reduce the amount of work involved simply by choosing low-maintenance plants and keeping them weed-free by mulching, perhaps with a decorative chipped bark, or with chemical controls. Whatever planting style you choose avoid using plants that grow rampantly, need constant cutting back or frequent pruning, and any with lots of seeds that germinate readily where you don't want them to.

Above: Foliage plants create colour and interest but require very little attention through the year.

Foliage

Interesting foliage often acts as a backdrop to flowers, but it can also be used on its own. The enormous range of greens as well as purples, bronzes, silvers and striking variegations makes it entirely possible to create unusual effects using foliage alone.

Evergreens are especially useful because they don't shed leaves like deciduous shrubs do or die down leaving dead matter to be cleared away as do perennials. However, deciduous shrubs produce some stunning autumn effects, which are particularly useful when the number of flowers is declining in your border.

Incorporating Flowers

However attractive foliage may be, for most people a garden would not be complete without flowers. Happily, many will perform well with little attention, and there are a number of different types of flowering plants to choose from.

Above: Packed borders require little weeding once established.

Above: If you want to include summer bedding plants in your border choose a long-flowering type, such as geraniums.

Traditional seasonal borders are replanted twice a year with bedding plants to take full advantage of spring and summer flower colour. They are packed with colour but require most work and are best avoided if you have limited time. Using more permanent plants instead will involve less time.

Annuals are less work for the gardener as many can be sown in situ. They are invaluable for filling gaps with bright summer colour. You sow them in late spring and they flower in summer, and many will self-seed for years. Pot marigolds, nasturtiums, love-in-a-mist, and different types of poppy, including Californian and common field poppies, are all good self-seeders. Any seedlings that appear in the wrong place can simply be pulled up. When the plants have finished flowering they can be removed.

With many different growth habits, sizes and flower shapes and colours, herbaceous perennials bring an extra dimension into a garden. Choose those that you can plant and forget, at least for a few years. They will flower year after year.

Shrubs are among the best plants for borders. Most will grow for years without any attention, but those that grow too vigorously (such as buddlejas and many roses) or that are tall and difficult to manage (such as lilacs) are best avoided. Fortunately, there are so many well-behaved shrubs, that a low-maintenance border is easy to achieve. Potentillas flower for months, as do hardy fuchsias, though these may be partly cut down in cold winter. Mahonia and hebe are also reliable.

Above: Papaver somniferum *will self-seed on to any bare patches of soil in a border.*

31

Herbaceous Borders

Whole borders devoted to herbaceous perennials look stunning during the summer months and well into autumn. Plants like astilbes, dicentras and bergenias, which need no staking, spread relatively slowly and are easy to pull up when necessary, are ideal. If you are in doubt about a plant's suitability, always find out whether it needs staking, how fast it spreads and whether it is prone to pests and diseases. Phlox and perennial asters are prone to mildew, for example.

Mixed Borders

These contain a mixture of shrubs for structure and foliage and perennial plants, perhaps supplemented by annuals. Generally, they require less maintenance than herbaceous borders, especially if the emphasis is on low-maintenance shrubs, with some easy perennials to add colour.

When you plant the border, you will need to leave gaps to allow shrubs and perennials to grow. The gaps can be temporarily filled with annuals such as marigolds, poppies or nasturtiums, or bedding plants such as geraniums or begonias. This will keep down the weeds and look good.

Above: Self-sufficient spurge, purple sage, lavender and iris pack a mixed border with colour.

Left: Attractive, low-maintenance perennials in a border can provide years of interest with their colourful flowers and variety of foliage.

PLANTING A BORDER

After initial planting, you will need to water the border regularly in dry periods until the plants are established, but thereafer they should need little attention to keep them looking good over a long period.

1 Water the plants, then arrange the pots in their planting places. Try to visualize the plants at their final height and spread, then adjust their positions, allowing room for growth. Dig the first hole, and add some well-rotted compost, farmyard manure or slow-release fertilizer.

> **RELIABLE AND EASY**
> **HERBACEOUS PERENNIALS**
> *Anemone* x *hybrida*
> *Anthemis tinctoria*
> *Astilbe*
> *Bergenia*
> *Dianthus*
> *Dicentra spectabilis*
> *Echinops ritro*
> *Erigeron*
> *Hemerocallis*
> *Kniphofia*
> *Liriope muscari*
> *Rudbeckia*
> *Schizostylis coccinea*
> *Sedum spectabile*
> *Tradescantia*
> *Veronica spicata*

2 When you are ready to plant, knock a plant out of its pot and tease out some of the roots. Start at the back, or at one end of the border.

3 Return the soil and make sure the plant is at its original depth or just a little deeper. Firm it with your hands or a heel to expel large pockets of air in the soil and prevent wind rock. Water thoroughly unless the weather is wet.

Above: The several varieties of Sedum *provide pinks and reds in autumn. They require practically no attention and do not need staking.*

Low-maintenance Plants

PLANTS THAT REQUIRE LITTLE ATTENTION THROUGH THE YEAR AND ARE GENERALLY DISEASE- AND PEST-RESISTANT ARE THE ONES TO INCLUDE IN A LOW-MAINTENANCE GARDEN. THERE IS ENOUGH CHOICE TO ENSURE INTEREST AND PLENTY OF COLOUR AT ALL TIMES.

Left: Stipa tenuifolia *produces silky flowerheads that sway sensuously in summer breezes.*

reach 2.4m (8ft) or more. They can be used in beds, either on their own or in mixed plantings, to stunning effect.

Be cautious about mixing grasses among other plants, however, as some are difficult to control, and rampant species will soon take over a bed and become inextricably entwined with other plants, so clump-forming types are best. The more spreading grasses are better grown in an isolated spot, but the smaller ones will work in a border if you plant them in a large container sunk into the ground, with the rim flush with the surrounding soil. Annual grasses will self-seed unless you deadhead them after flowering.

GRACEFUL GRASSES FOR YEAR-ROUND INTEREST

Perennial grasses are easy plants. Once planted, they require very little attention, except occasional removal of dead foliage and old flower heads if they offend. Cutting back the dead foliage to ground level in early spring will encourage lots of new growth.

There are many types to grow, from compact dwarfs to huge plants that

GRASSES

Andropogon
Carex
Cortaderia selloana
Deschampsia
Festuca glauca
Hakonechloa
Miscanthus sinensis
Stipa arundinacea
Stipa tenuifolia

FERNS FOR MOIST SHADE

The intricate foliage of ferns makes these fascinating plants essential for moist, shady corners of any low-maintenance garden, where they will thrive without any intervention. Many die down in winter, but there are also plenty of evergreen species, and they are varied enough in shape and size to make an interesting planting despite the lack of flowers.

Above: Ferns can be used very effectively to soften a focal point like this ornament in a dull corner of the garden. They require little attention.

FERNS

Adiantum (some evergreen)
Asplenium ceterach (evergreen)
Asplenium scolopendrium
(evergreen)
Blechnum capense (evergreen)
Dryopteris affinis 'Cristata'
(evergreen)
Polypodium (some evergreen)
Polystichum setiferum (evergreen)

PLANTING FERNS

Most ferns prefer a moist, shady or partially shaded position, and will do especially well if you take time to prepare the soil by incorporating plenty of organic material. This is very important in an area shaded by a tree or wall, where soil is usually dry. If the soil is impoverished, rake a balanced fertilizer into the surface of the soil when you plant. If planting in late summer, autumn or winter do not use a quick-acting fertilizer.

1 Water the fern thoroughly about half an hour before planting. It is very important that ferns do not dry out, especially when newly planted.

2 Make a hole large enough to take the rootball. Firm the fern in carefully. Then water thoroughly so that the surrounding soil is moist down to the depth of the rootball.

3 To help conserve moisture and maintain a high level of organic material in the soil, mulch thickly. Top up the mulch each spring.

HEATHERS FOR CARPETS OF COLOUR

Robust heathers make excellent low-maintenance beds in open sunny positions. There are varieties to provide year-round colour and most have attractive foliage, which often changes colour according to the season.

If you have space, heathers look best planted in bold drifts. Depending on the size of the bed, plant them in groups of perhaps ten or twenty of each variety. If you make your selection with care, you can have some in flower in virtually every season of the year. They can also be used in combination with conifers to create striking effects.

Limited Maintenance

The only attention heathers need is an annual trim in mid-spring; cut out old flowerheads as well as any dead, diseased or damaged shoots. Apply a slow-release fertilizer after pruning.

Heathers can become woody with time and may require replacing after some years.

Above: A carpet of heathers is a glorious sight. Mix varieties that flower at different times for year-round interest.

PLANTING HEATHERS

Make sure you choose the correct type of heathers for your soil. Winter-flowering *Erica carnea* varieties, which are more correctly known as heaths, will grow on neutral or even slightly alkaline soil. True heathers, such as *Erica cinerea* and *Calluna vulgaris* varieties, need an acid soil. When planting, it is important to prepare the soil thoroughly, and adding peat to the planting area will benefit all types. Plant through a sheet of black plastic or a plastic mulching sheet to keep weeding down to the absolute minimum. Then you can mulch on top of the sheet with a more attractive material such as chipped bark or gravel.

1 Prepare the soil thoroughly before planting. Add plenty of organic material such as compost or well-rotted manure, especially if the soil is dry or impoverished of nutrients. If planting in spring or summer, rake in a balanced general fertilizer. If planting in autumn or winter, wait until spring to apply fertilizer to avoid scorching tender roots.

2 Start planting at one end or at the back of the bed. Space the plants about 30–45cm (12–18in) apart. The planting distance will vary according to the species and even variety, so check first. Plant with a trowel and press the soil down firmly with your hands to exclude any air pockets.

3 Use a mulch of peat or composted chipped bark to suppress weeds, conserve moisture, and improve the appearance of the soil while the plants are still young. Over time this will rot down and provide nutrients for the growing plants and may need topping up every few years.

HEATHERS
Calluna vulgaris
Daboecia cantabrica
Erica carnea
Erica ciliaris
Erica cinerea
Erica x *darleyensis*
Erica erigena
Erica mackaiana
Erica tetralix
Erica vagans

ARCHITECTURAL CONIFERS

Slow-growing conifers need little attention after their first year, as long as they are given a good start with careful site preparation and planting.

Dwarf and slow-growing conifers can be columnar, rounded, oval or prostrate in outline, and to look effective they are best grown as a group with contrasting shapes, sizes and colours. They are ideal for small beds or borders where they will soon provide year-round interest.

Planting Conifers

If you find it difficult to plan beds and borders on paper, stand the pots where you think the plants will look good and be prepared to shuffle them around until they look right. Bear in mind the eventual height and spread.

Dig a hole larger and deeper than the rootball, and fork in rotted manure, garden compost or planting mixture, especially on dry soils, then work in a controlled- or slow-release fertilizer. Mulch with a decorative material at least 5cm (2in) thick.

Above: Slow-growing conifers provide year-round colour.

Left: Dwarf conifers look good in a group. Before planting check how they will look together and make any necessary adjustments to their positions.

Above: Surround newly planted conifers and heathers with decorative organic mulch such as chipped bark.

HEATHER AND CONIFER BEDS

Dwarf conifers combine especially well with heathers, their foliage providing fascinating contrasts of texture and colour. There are hundreds of suitable heathers and conifers so you can design exactly what you want. Remember to choose varieties that are suitable for your soil type. The initial outlay may seem expensive, but the bed should last for a long time without the need for replanting and will require minimal maintenance.

DWARF CONIFERS

Abies cephalonica
'Meyer's Dwarf'
Chamaecyparis obtusa
'Nana Gracilis'
Picea abies 'Gregoryana'
Taxus baccata 'Standishii'
Thuja picata 'Irish Gold'

Planting a Mixed Bed

Arrange and plant all the conifers first, making sure they look pleasing from all angles. Space the heathers around the conifers, then plant them in groups or drifts of one variety at a time. Avoid planting the heathers too close to the conifers as all the plants will spread and merge into each other within a year or two. Meanwhile cover the bare soil with chipped bark or gravel.

Above: Conifers and heathers make a natural combination in this setting.

TIME-SAVING BEDDING PLANTS

Traditional summer bedding involves a lot of time and work. Even if you buy all the plants from a nursery to avoid the annual rituals of sowing, labelling and potting on, they still have to be planted out in the garden. However, if you like the instant cheerful brightness of seasonal bedding rather than the predictable show from shrubs and border plants, you can compromise by mixing a temporary selection of seasonal bedding with established planting. The bedding plants will add splashes of bright, long-lasting summer colour among the more permanent plants. A low-growing perennial, such as sedum, can be used as a neat year-round edging that requires at the most an annual trim to keep it looking tidy. The centre of the bed can then be filled with spring bulbs and summer bedding plants.

TROUBLE-FREE SUMMER BEDDING PLANTS

Begonia semperflorens
Impatiens
Lavatera trimestris
Osteospermum
Pelargonium
Petunia
Tagetes patula

If you choose bedding plants such as begonias or petunias that flower prolifically over a long period without much attention, you will further cut down on the amount of work involved. The plants listed above will continue to flower for many months without requiring deadheading, regular attention or watering. They are some of the most trouble-free and spectacular bedding plants you can use.

Below: Impatiens *and* Begonia *'White Devil' (right) are two long-flowering and reliable summer bedding plants.*

PLANTING A PERMANENT EDGING

If you want to add small permanent plants at the front of a border that will give seasonal splashes of colour rather than temporary bedding plants choose from the wide range of miniature bulbs or creeping plants.

1 Dig over the ground at the front of the border and clear it of weeds. Rake in a general fertilizer if planting in spring to encourage vigorous early growth and help the plants to knit together. (Wait until spring to do this if planting in autumn or winter.)

2 Space the plants out in their pots and adjust them to go evenly around the bed. About 15cm (6in) apart is suitable for most plants if you want quick cover, further apart if you don't mind waiting a little longer. Plant using a trowel.

3 Firm in to remove large pockets of air, then water thoroughly. The bed may be planted immediately with bulbs or spring or summer bedding plants as appropriate.

Above: Cyclamen *form a clump of variegated leaves, with bright flowers in late winter. They are particularly suited to the front of a shady border.*

PLANTS AND BULBS FOR PERMANENT EDGING

Creeping willow
Cyclamen
Dianthus
Grape hyacinth
Lavandula 'Munstead Dwarf'
Miniature box
Salvia officinalis

Above: Creeping willow is an excellent plant for permanent edging with its delicate, glossy green foliage and attractive yellow flowers.

SELF-SUFFICIENT SHRUBS

Some of the most popular shrubs, like roses and buddlejas, require a lot of attention. Regular pruning is necessary for many of them to remain looking good, and others may be prone to pests and diseases, which require time and effort to prevent or eliminate. Fortunately, there are many low-maintenance shrubs that are just as attractive and almost trouble-free.

You can choose from hundreds of well-behaved compact shrubs that will not require frequent pruning or hacking back. Check with your local garden centre to make sure the shrubs you select won't need regular pruning, won't become bare and leggy at the base with all the flowers at the top, and aren't susceptible to diseases.

Viburnum tinus is useful for its autumn and winter flowers, but it can

Above: Easy to grow Elaeagnus *is an ideal low-maintenance shrub. Its silvery foliage is set off by* Erysimum.

grow tall and require pruning to keep it compact. Many hebes are naturally compact and so require little pruning; most have pretty flowers, but some need protection during cold winters.

Above: Compact and evergreen hebes need protection where winters are severe.

LOW-MAINTENANCE SHRUBS

Flowering
Cistus
Escallonia
Hibiscus syriacus
Hypericum
Mahonia
Olearia x *hastii*
Yucca

Foliage
Aucuba japonica
Berberis thunbergii
Choisya ternata
Elaeagnus pungens 'Maculata'
Euonymus fortunei
Ruscus aculeatus
Viburnum davidii

Above: Choisya ternata *has the benefit of a strong shape, pale green foliage and delightfully scented white flowers.*

PLANTING SHRUBS

Your choice of shrubs will be in position for many years, so plant them carefully and take time to prepare the ground thoroughly.

Water the pots and let them drain. Position them where you think they should be in the border. Check the likely size on the label or in a book, then revise your spacing if necessary. If the spacing seems excessive initially, leaving large gaps, you can always plant a few extra inexpensive shrubs between them to discard when they become crowded.

If planting in spring or summer, apply a balanced fertilizer according to the manufacturer's instructions; if planting at any other time, wait until spring to apply. Hoe or rake it into the surface then water thoroughly.

1 Dig a hole large enough to take the rootball. Stand the plant in the hole and use a cane or stick to check that the plant will be at the same depth as it was in the pot. Add or remove soil as necessary.

2 Carefully tease out some of the roots if they are tightly wound round the inside of the pot. This will encourage them to grow out into the surrounding soil and become quickly established.

3 Return the soil and firm it well around the roots to steady the shrub in wind and to eliminate large pockets of air that might allow the roots to dry out. Keep it watered during dry periods to begin with; once established, it should rarely require watering.

SELF-SEEDING FLOWERS

Plants that self-seed freely around the garden can be a nuisance if they germinate in the wrong place, because then you have to spend time pulling them up. However, if they are in the right place they can be a labour-saving boon to the gardener.

You will have to sow self-seeders initially, of course. Decide on a position where the plants can multiply freely without becoming a nuisance. Suitable places are among shrubs and herbaceous plants, especially in a mixed bed, or in beds restrained by clear boundaries, such as a bed in a lawn. Sow only into well-prepared ground that is completely free of weeds. You may have to weed twice initially to ensure clear soil.

Above: Limnanthes douglasii *(poached egg plant) is one of the easiest self-sowing plants.*

SELF-SOWING PLANTS

Annuals
Calendula
Eschscholzia
Limnanthes
Lunaria

Perennials
Aquilegia
Digitalis
Foeniculum vulgare
Lupinus

Maintenance of Self-sown Plants

After initial sowing, and each subsequent year, pull out any weed seedlings before they compete with the sown seedlings. You should be able to identify the desirable seedlings by the larger number with the same kind of leaf. As the seedlings become larger, hoe between them to control weeds. Once the plants meet, you should be able to stop weeding.

Where seedlings have self-sown too thickly, you may need to thin the plants in spring.

Above: Fennel *(*Foeniculum vulgare) *has very tall delicate feathery fronds in green or bronze.*

Sowing Seed In Situ

1 Scatter annuals randomly. Avoid sowing too thickly, otherwise you will have more thinning to do. Rake the seeds in, first in one direction and then in the other direction if possible.

2 Sow perennials such as lupins and columbines in small pinches about 45cm (28in) apart. Rake some soil over the seeds.

3 Keep the seeds watered until they germinate and are growing well. If there are spaces between plants you could fill the gaps with a decorative mulch to suppress weeds. You will need to thin the plants out if a group have germinated together.

Above: *Self-sowing honesty (*Lunaria annua) *provides purple or white flowers and attractive papery seed heads.*

Above: *The bright orange flowers of pot marigolds (*Calendula officinalis) *contrast wonderfully with silver and grey shrubs. As well as being an attractive addition to the border the petals make a tasty ingredient in a summer salad.*

45

LOW-MAINTENANCE BULBS

Producing flower colour for virtually any time of the year, bulbs make a valuable contribution to the low-maintenance garden. Many bulbs will flower reliably year after year, with the clumps improving all the time, and once they have been planted they need very little attention.

Most summer-flowering bulbs, such as alliums and lilies, are best planted in groups in a border, but the easiest way to grow many spring- and autumn-flowering bulbs is to naturalize them in grass. This eliminates the need for annual replanting and means that you don't have to cut that part of the lawn until the leaves have died down naturally. It is better to keep naturalized bulbs to one small area of the lawn so that the rest can be cut normally and it won't look too untidy.

Caring for Bulbs

Naturalized bulbs and those left in a border for many years will eventually need dividing to prevent overcrowding, which would lead to deteriorating results. Lift large clumps when the leaves have just died back, or any time when the bulbs are dormant. Separate the clump into smaller pieces and replant. You do not have to separate into individual bulbs.

Above: A sunny border aglow with yellow tulips will give pleasure year after year.

Left: Daffodils naturalized in a small area of lawn look charming in the early spring.

NATURALIZING LARGE BULBS

1 To create a natural effect, scatter the bulbs on the grass and plant them where they fall. Make a hole for each, roughly three times their own depth, using either a trowel or a bulb planter, which pulls out a neat plug of grass and soil. Insertion will be easier if the ground is moist rather than dry.

EASY BULBS
Allium
Colchicum
Crocus
Cyclamen
Galanthus nivalis
Lilium
Muscari
Narcissus
Tulipa

2 Place a bulb in the hole. Crumble some soil from the bottom of the plug and let it fall around the bulb to make sure it will not be left in a pocket of air. Press the plug back into position.

Above: Autumn-flowering Colchicum *extend the interest in a bulb filled lawn.*

NATURALIZING SMALL BULBS

1 For small bulbs and corms it is sometimes easier to lift and then replace the grass. Use a spade to slice beneath the grass, then roll it back for planting.

2 Loosen the soil with a fork, and work in a slow-acting fertilizer such as bonemeal. Scatter the bulbs randomly as a uniform pattern will look unnatural in grass. Small ones can be left on the surface; larger ones are best buried slightly.

3 Aim to cover the bulbs with twice their own depth of soil under the grass. Roll back the grass, firm it well with your hands and water thoroughly.

TIME-SAVING GROUND COVER

Plants that cover bare ground with a carpet of colour are invaluable in the low-maintenance garden, not least for their ability to suppress weeds. They are ideal for softening the hard edges of a path or the front of borders and for filling in gaps.

Ground-cover plants usually grow no more than 45cm (18in) in height, but many shrubs and sub-shrubs are compact enough to be used as ground cover as well. Heathers and conifers make pleasing ground cover, although the latter may be slow growing. Prostrate cotoneasters make excellent ground-hugging cover in front of other shrubs. Many prostrate thymes are also good ground covers.

Some herbaceous plants make a carpet of lush foliage in summer, as well as flowers in many cases. Hostas, for instance, have a wide range of leaf

Above: Hostas make excellent ground cover in moist, shady areas.

colour and delicate spears of pale lilac or white flowers, while cranesbills bloom for a long period.

Some ground-covering shrubs, such as *Hypericum calycinum*, are normally too aggressive for a small garden and will quickly take over. But this hypericum is ideal for a sloping bank that is difficult to cultivate. (If you plant it elsewhere you will need to contain it with paving.)

Left: Euonymus fortunei *'Emerald 'n' Gold' makes a striking ground cover in sun or shade. Its brightly variegated leaves will provide winter colour.*

Left: Lamium maculatum *is quick to become established and makes an effective and colourful ground cover in spring.*

> **GROUND-COVERING PLANTS**
>
> *Ajuga reptans*
> *Alchemilla mollis*
> *Bergenia*
> *Cerastium tomentosum*
> *Convallaria majalis*
> *Geranium endressii*
> *Hypericum calycinum*
> *Lamium maculatum*
> *Pulmonaria*
> *Tiarella cordifolia*
> *Vinca minor*

Filling Shady Locations

Fast-growing ivy is excellent for all types of shade, and *Pachysandra terminalis* 'Variegata' makes a green-and-white carpet in dry shade. Lily-of-the-valley, *Liriope muscari* and periwinkle also grow well below trees.

Maintenance of Ground Cover

Many ground-cover plants are quite tough, and once planted require little attention other than an annual feed. Heathers need an annual trim with shears after flowering to keep them looking neat. And plants like *Hypericum calycinum* can be clipped annually with shears or a nylon line trimmer to reduce their height and encourage bushiness.

Planting Ground-cover Plants

Ground cover will eventually suppress weeds, but initially needs protection from them. Before you start planting, clear the ground thoroughly of existing weeds.

Unless you are planting a ground cover that spreads by underground stems or rooting prostrate stems on the surface, it is best to plant through a mulching sheet to control weeds while the plants are becoming established. If you are planting large ground-cover plants, you may need to dig holes with a spade before laying the mulching sheet.

Above: Evergreen ivy is a fast-growing plant for ground cover.

Making the Most of Trees

Trees make attractive features as specimens set in a lawn, or planted towards the back of a shrub border. Once they are established, most trees require no maintenance. Those in a border are generally less trouble because falling leaves drop almost unnoticed onto the soil, where they are quickly recycled.

Make your selection to suit the size of your garden and to give as much long-term interest as possible. Many small ornamental trees bear spring blossom, or have bright autumn foliage such as *Acer palmatum*, or they may have berries or fruit, including many varieties of *Malus*. Some have interestingly coloured or textured bark, which stands out in winter; the peeling bark of *Acer griseum*, for instance, is cinnamon-coloured.

SMALL GARDEN TREES
Acer palmatum
Crataegus
Malus
Prunus
Sorbus vilmorinii

Trees in Lawns

Leaves on a lawn usually have to be raked up, but a way around this problem could be to choose a tree with small leaves or an evergreen one. Mowing beneath a low-hanging tree or up to a trunk can also cause difficulties. Lawn trees are generally better planted in a bed cut into the grass, which can either be planted with attractive ground cover or covered with a decorative mulch to suppress weeds and retain moisture.

Trees in Borders

The best way to cover the ground beneath trees in a border is with ground-cover plants that will tolerate shade and dry soil. If the tree is very large or has large leaves you may have to rake the leaves off the plants when they fall, but most of them usually work their way between the plants and soon rot down. If you use a ground cover that dies down in winter, falling leaves will not matter.

Left: Mulch around the base of a specimen tree to prevent weed growth. Large pebbles have been used here but you could also choose chipped bark or gravel.

PLANTING A LAWN TREE

1 Mark a circle on the grass about 90–120cm (3–4ft) across. Lift the grass with a spade, and remove about 5cm (6in) of soil with it. Dig a planting hole, and fork in plenty of garden compost or well-rotted manure.

2 Insert a short but sturdy wooden stake before you plant the tree, placing it on the side of the prevailing wind. Place it off-centre, to allow space for the large rootball.

3 Place the tree in the hole and use a cane to check that the final soil level – about 5cm (2in) below the grass – will be the same as in the container (or with bare-root trees the soil mark on the stem).

4 With bare-root trees, spread out the roots; with container-grown ones, gently tease some out. Return the soil, and firm in well. Water thoroughly, secure with a tree-tie, and mulch the bed.

Above: This magnificent magnolia is underplanted with grape hyacinths. The colours look stunning when both are in flower.

51

Ideas for Special Features

Some of the most popular garden features can also be low-maintenance if selected wisely and carefully established. Here are some suggestions for installing and maintaining a selection of attractive additions to your garden.

Easy-care Containers

The main task with containers is watering, which in summer often needs to be done more than once a day. However, an automatic watering system can take care of this.

Alternatively, choose tough plants such as shrubs, rather than bedding plants. They will still need watering, but will survive limited periods of neglect. There are also perennial plants that can remain in their containers for several years. These will provide less of a summer show than brightly coloured bedding plants, but can be successful as focal points.

Mixed Collections

Try a mixed planting of perhaps three small shrubs, with different foliage shapes and colours. If you really want the brightness of bedding plants, plant just a couple of these and have permanent plants in other containers.

Decorative Containers

Some flowering evergreens can look a bit boring when not in bloom. A frost-proof decorative pot will make sure such plants always remain a feature.

> EASY-CARE PLANTS
> FOR CONTAINERS
>
> *Azalea*
> *Bergenia*
> Dwarf conifers
> *Erica hyemalis*
> *Euonymus fortunei*
> 'Emerald 'n' Gold'
> *Fatsia japonica*
> *Gaultheria*
> *Hebe*
> *Phormium*
> *Rhododendron*
> *Santolina chamaecyparissus*
> *Skimmia*

Left: *A collection of shrubs, conifers and bergenia has plenty of impact. They won't die if left unwatered for a day or two.*

WATER FEATURES

If you like water features, installing a fountain or pond are simple ways to create an interesting low-maintenance garden. A large pond may be less demanding than a flowerbed.

How to Make a Pond

Make your pond as large as possible. Fish and wildlife will be happier, and the water will stay clearer. You can dig out a pond and line it in a weekend, but you may prefer to get someone else to excavate it for you. Leave a shallow ledge 23cm (9in) down around part of the pond for marginal plants, and to allow wildlife access.

Planting a Pond

The best time to plant aquatics is spring and early summer, so that they

> **TROUBLE-FREE PLANTS FOR PONDS**
>
> *Acorus graminens* 'Variegatus'
> *Aponegeton distachysos*
> *Iris laevigata* (Japanese iris)
> *Myriphyllum aquaticum*
> *Pontederia cordata*

can become established. Use a planting basket designed for aquatic plants, line it with a special basket liner and use aquatic soil.

Maintenance

Overcrowded plants benefit from division and replanting in spring, and in autumn it's best to cut down dead foliage that might pollute the water, and to rake out the leaves. Every few years the pond should be emptied and cleaned – the only big task.

Above: *A pond can become a strong focal point, yet the amount of maintenance required is modest.*

HEDGES

Well-clipped hedges are excellent plants for defining and giving structure to a garden, and for many gardeners a hedge is preferable to a fence or wall. However, hedges can be tedious and time-consuming to trim. Nonetheless with imagination you may be able to overcome some of the problems.

Down-sizing

Many established hedges will respond well to quite severe height or width reduction, which will cut down considerably on the amount of trimming required. Cut back to about 30cm (12in) lower or in from the final height or width, to allow for new growth. Improving the shape of a straight-sided hedge by sloping the sides will marginally reduce the amount to be cut and make pruning easier.

LOW- MAINTENANCE HEDGES
Beech
Carpinus betulus
Ilex
Laurel
Ligistrum
Taxus Baccata

Alternative Plants

Think about using low-maintenance plants if you are planting a new hedge. It may even be worth replacing a rather boring or very formal hedge with a more easily maintained and attractive alternative. Informal flowering hedges only need cutting back once a year after flowering, whereas formal hedges usually require clipping two or three times a year to look good. A beech or hornbeam hedge requires only one clip a year, in late summer.

Above: *A mature beech hedge will need trimming only once a year.*

Above: A Clematis *'Bees' Jubilee' scrambling over a rhododendron will flower after its host has finished.*

CLIMBERS

Although climbers are popular for softening walls and fences, many require regular pruning, training or tying which can be time-consuming. However, many climbers are self-clinging or twining, so do not need tying in. Roses do need regular pruning to flower well, and many plants benefit from dead-heading, but most climbers will perform well if simply pruned when they outgrow their allotted space.

Planting a Climber

1 Make the planting hole at least 45cm (1½ft) away from a wall or fence, to avoid the "rain shadow" that will prevent moisture reaching young roots. Work plenty of moisture-holding material such as garden compost or manure into the soil.

2 Plant at an angle so that the stems grow towards the wall. Leave in any cane that was used as a support while in the pot, but if there are several stems untie them and spread them out.

3 To help start off newly planted self-clinging plants, use small ties that you can fix to the wall by suction or a special adhesive.

4 Water thoroughly after planting and whenever the ground is dry during the first season. Once the plant is well established, watering should seldom be necessary.

SELF-CLINGING AND
TWINING CLIMBERS

Ceropegia sandersonii
Clematis
Hedera
Lonicera periclymenum
Manettia leuteorubra
Parthenocissus quinquefolia
Tropaeolum
Wisteria sinensis

A Simplified Kitchen Garden

Kitchen gardens are usually labour-intensive, with many hours spent digging, watering, feeding and weeding. If you want to grow fruit and vegetables in a low-maintenance garden, choose those that demand the least attention and try some of the techniques described here.

Watering Edible Plants

Vegetables and salads need plenty of water, so a sprinkler will be essential. To save more time, you could add a time switch to make the system automatic. Seep hoses are ideal for rows of vegetables as the water goes directly to where it is needed at the roots (see Easy Garden Maintenance).

Above: Planting fruit and vegetable seedlings through a mulching sheet will avoid the need for weeding.

Eliminate Weeding

By using a mulching sheet that will keep out light yet let through water, you can almost eliminate weeding on beds. Always make sure the soil is enriched with well-rotted manure or garden compost and fertilizers before you lay the mulching sheet. Secure the sheet edges, then cut crosses in the sheet with a knife and plant through the holes, folding the sheet back after planting. Water thoroughly. Later, feeding is best done by applying a liquid fertilizer, rather than compost, so that it will penetrate the mulch to reach the plant roots.

Above: French beans need a rich soil but require little after-care, apart from regular harvesting to maintain production.

GARDENER'S TIP

If you find spacing seeds by hand difficult, one of the proprietary seed-sowers might help. These are available for both seed trays and drills. For sowing in the ground, you can choose a long-handled version, to avoid the need for bending.

Growing Fruit

Concentrate on soft fruit such as blackcurrants and raspberries. Gooseberries are trouble-free in themselves but are prone to pests and diseases. Rhubarb is completely trouble-free. You can leave it for years, to flourish without any attention at all.

Avoid troublesome fruit such as apricots, which are demanding, and apples and pears, which are prone to problems and require careful pruning if trained to one of the systems popular in small gardens.

If you really want to grow apples, try one of the flagpoles that grow upright and form the fruit on natural short spurs along the upright stem. Apart from cutting out the odd wayward shoot, pruning is not required.

Above: This eye-catching herb and salad garden is easy to maintain.

Growing Vegetables and Salad

There are many vegetables and salads that are easy to grow and are not overly troubled by pests and diseases. Many can now be bought as plugs from the garden centre if you do not want to sow them from seed. Try courgettes, French beans, sweetcorn, perpetual spinach, lettuces and rocket. If you enjoy the taste of home-grown new potatoes, but do not want all the hard work of earthing up several times and heavy digging to harvest, you can grow them beneath black polythene.

Above: Potatoes grown under black polythene are easy to cultivate and harvest as they do not require earthing up.

Growing Herbs

After the initial soil preparation to provide well-drained conditions, many herbs are easy to grow. If you stick to perennials such as chives, sage, rosemary, thyme, French tarragon and winter savory, the only maintenance required is regular picking to prevent flowering and cutting down in the autumn or early spring to encourage new growth.

Easy-care Plants

USE THIS LIST OF EASY-CARE PLANTS TO PLAN YOUR GARDEN SO THAT IT REQUIRES MINIMUM MAINTENANCE.

Plant Name	When to Plant	Season of Interest
Acer palmatum (s)	autumn	autumn foliage
Ajuga reptans (ps, fs)	autumn, spring	year-round
Allium (s)	autumn	summer, autumn
Anemone x *hybrida* (s, ps)	spring	late summer to mid-autumn
Anthemis tinctoria (s)	autumn, spring	summer
Aquilegia (s, ps)	autumn, spring	late spring, early summer
Artemisia absinthium (s)	autumn, spring	late summer
Astilbe (s)	autumn, spring	summer
Aucuba japonica (s, ps, fs)	autumn	year-round
Azalea * (ps)	autumn	spring
Begonia semperflorens ñ (ps)	late spring	summer
Berberis (s, ps)	autumn	spring, autumn
Bergenia (s, ps)	autumn, spring	spring
Buxus sempervirens (ps)	autumn	year-round
Calendula officinalis (s, ps)	sow in situ, spring	summer to autumn
Calluna vulgaris * (s)	autumn, spring	summer, autumn
Carex (s, ps)	autumn, spring	year-round
Chamaecyparis, dwarf cultivars ñ to slightly ^ (s)	autumn, spring	year-round
Chamaemelum nobile 'Treneague' (s)	sow in situ or divide in spring	year-round
Choisya ternata (s)	autumn, spring	year-round
Cistus (s)	autumn, spring	summer

Allium

Calendula

Colchicum autumnale (s)	summer	autumn
Cortaderia selloana (s)	autumn, spring	late summer
Cotoneaster (s, ps)	autumn	year-round, autumn berries
Crataegus (s, ps)	autumn	spring flowers, autumn fruits
Crocus (s)	autumn, summer	spring, autumn
Cyclamen (ps)	late summer	autumn, winter, early spring
Cytisus (s)	autumn	summer
Deschampsia ñ to * (s, ps)	autumn, spring	late spring, early summer
Dianthus ñ to ^ (s)	autumn, spring	summer
Dicentra spectabilis ñ to ^ (ps)	autumn, spring	summer
Digitalis purpurea (ps)	autumn	late spring, early summer
Echinops ritro (s, ps)	autumn	early summer
Elaeagnus pungens (s, ps)	autumn	summer
Erica cultivars * (s)	autumn	winter, spring
Erigeron (ps)	autumn	spring, summer
Eryngium (s)	spring, autumn	summer
Eschscholzia californica (s)	sow in situ, spring	summer to autumn
Euonymus fortunei (s)	autumn	year-round
Euphorbia (s)	autumn	summer
Fatsia japonica (s, ps)	autumn	year-round
Festuca glauca (s)	autumn, winter	year-round
Galanthus nivalis (ps)	autumn	late winter, early spring
*Gaultheria (*syn. *Pernettya)* * to ñ (ps)	autumn	year-round
Geranium (s, ps)	spring, autumn	summer
Hakonechloa (s, ps)	spring, autumn	year-round
Hebe (s, ps)	autumn	year-round, summer flowers
Hedera (s, ps, fs)	autumn	year-round
Helichrysum ñ to ^ (s)	autumn	summer, autumn
Hemerocallis (s)	autumn	summer
Hosta (ps, fs)	autumn	summer

Deschampsia

Erica *cultivars*

Houttuynia cordata (s)	autumn, spring	spring, summer
Hypericum calycinum (s, ps)	autumn	summer
Ilex aquifolium (s)	autumn, spring	year-round, autumn berries
Impatiens (ps)	autumn, spring	spring to autumn
Juniperus horizontalis (s)	autumn	year-round
Kniphofia hybrids (s, ps)	autumn, spring	summer
Lamium maculatum (ps, s)	spring, autumn	summer to autumn
Lavandula (s)	autumn	summer, early autumn
Lavatera trimestris (s)	autumn, spring	summer
Laurus nobilis (s, ps)	autumn	year-round
Lilium * (s, ps)	autumn, spring	summer
Limnanthes (s)	sow in situ, spring	summer
Liriope muscari (fs)	autumn	autumn
Lonicera periclymenum (s, ps)	autumn	summer
Lupinus slightly * (s, ps)	autumn, spring	summer
Mahonia (fs)	autumn, spring	autumn, winter, spring
Malus (s, ps)	autumn	spring, autumn fruits
Miscanthus sinensis (s)	autumn	spring to autumn
Muscari (s)	autumn	spring
Narcissus (s)	autumn	spring
Olearia x *haastii* (s)	autumn	year-round, summer flowers
Origanum vulgare ^ (s)	autumn	summer
Osteospermum (s)	spring	summer
Parthenocissus quinquefolia (s, fs)	autumn, spring	spring to autumn
Pelargonium (s)	spring	summer
Persicaria affinis (s, ps)	spring	summer to autumn
Petunia (s)	spring	summer to autumn
Phormium (s)	autumn, spring	year-round
Pyracantha (s, ps)	spring, autumn	autumn berries
Rhododendron *(ps)	autumn, spring	late spring
Rosmarinus officinalis (s)	autumn	year-round

Lavandula

Juniperus horizontalis

Rudbeckia (s)	autumn, spring	summer to autumn
Salvia officinalis (s)	autumn	year-round
Santolina chamaecyparissus (s)	autumn, spring	year-round, summer flowers
Schizostylis coccinea (s)	spring, autumn	summer, autumn
Sedum spectabile (s)	autumn	late summer
Sorbus vilmorinii (s)	autumn	autumn berries
Stipa (s)	autumn	year-round
Tagetes patula (s)	autumn, spring	summer to early autumn
Taxus baccata (s, ps, fs)	autumn	year-round, autumn berries
Thuja orientalis 'Aurea Nana' (s)	autumn, spring	year-round
Thymus ñ to ^ (s)	autumn, spring	year-round
Tropaeolum speciosum ñ to ^ (s, ps)	autumn	summer
Tulipa (s)	autumn	spring
Veronica spicata (s, ps)	autumn, spring	summer
Viburnum davidii (s, ps)	autumn	year-round
Vinca minor (s, ps)	autumn, spring	year-round
Waldsteinia ternata (ps, fs)	spring	mid- to late spring
Wisteria sinensis (s, ps)	autumn	summer
Yucca gloriosa (s)	spring	year-round

Stipa

Tulipa

SYMBOLS

Plants marked with * require acid soil;

Plants marked with ^ prefer alkaline soil;

Plants marked with ñ prefer neutral soil.

(S) = sun

(PS) = partial shade

(FS) = full shade

Common Names of Plants

bedding geranium
Pelargonium

beech *Fagus sylvatica*

box *Buxus sempervirens*

busy Lizzie *Impatiens*

Californian poppy
Eschscholzia

chamomile
Chamaemelum nobile

columbine *Aquilegia*

common bugle
Ajuga reptans

cowslip *Primula veris*

crab apple *Malus*

cranesbill *Geranium*

cuckoo flower
Cardamine pratensis

daffodil *Narcissus*

fennel *Foeniculum
vulgare*

flowering cherry *Prunus*

forget-me-not *Myosotis*

foxglove *Digitalis
purpurea*

French marigold
Tagetes patula

globe thistle *Echinops*

grape hyacinth *Muscari*

harebell *Campanula
rotundifolia*

hart's tongue fern
*Asplenium
scolopendrium*

heather *Calluna vulgaris*

hawthorn *Crataegus*

holly *Ilex aquifolium*

Above: *Large shrubs require limited maintenance.*

hornbeam *Carpinus
betulus*

ivy *Hedera*

Japanese maple
Acer palmatum

king fern *Dryopteris
pseudomas* 'Cristata'

lady fern *Athyrium*

lady's mantle *Alchemilla
mollis*

lily *Lilium*

lily-of-the-valley
Convallaria majalis

lupin *Lupinus*

lesser stitchwort *Stellaria
graminea*

meadow buttercup
Ranunculus acris

meadow cranesbill
Geranium pratense

milfoil *Achillea
millefolium*

periwinkle *Vinca minor*

pinks *Dianthus*

poached-egg plant
Limnanthes

pot marigold *Calendula*

rock rose *Cistus*

rose of Sharon *Hypericum
calycinum*

Rosemary *rosmarinus
officinalis*

sage *Salvia officinalis*

snake's-head fritillary
Fritillaria meleagris

Saint John's Wort
Hypericum

snowdrop *Galanthus
nivalis*

thyme *Thymus*

toadflax *Linaria*

tulip *Tulipa*

wild bergamot *Monarda
fistulosa*

winter heath *Erica
carnea*

yew *Taxus baccata*

Index

Above: An example of a minimalist garden.

Index

***Above:** Edging with large shrubs and small trees to reduce the size of a lawn.*